PENGUIN BOOKS

FEAR OF DESCRIPTION

Daniel Poppick's first book of poetry, *The Police*, was published by Omnidawn in 2017. His writing has appeared in *BOMB*, *Granta*, *The New Republic*, the Poetry Foundation's *PoetryNow* podcast, the PEN Poetry Series, and other journals. The recipient of awards from the MacDowell Colony and the Corporation of Yaddo and a graduate of the Iowa Writers' Workshop, he has taught writing at the University of Iowa, Coe College, and the Parsons School of Design. He currently lives in Brooklyn, where he works as a copywriter and coedits the Catenary Press.

THE NATIONAL POETRY SERIES

The National Poetry Series was established in 1978 to ensure the publication of five collections of poetry annually through five participating publishers. The Series is funded annually by Amazon Literary Partnership, the Gettinger Family Foundation, Bruce Gibney, HarperCollins Publishers, Stephen King, Lannan Foundation, Newman's Own Foundation, Anna and Olafur Olafsson, Penguin Random House, the Poetry Foundation, Elise and Steven Trulaske, and the National Poetry Series Board of Directors.

2018 COMPETITION WINNERS

Fear of Description
by Daniel Poppick of Brooklyn, NY,
chosen by Brenda Shaughnessy for Penguin Books

Valuing
by Christopher Kondrich of University Park, MD,
chosen by Jericho Brown for University of Georgia Press

Eyes Bottle Dark with a Mouthful of Flowers
by Jake Skeets of Vanderwagen, NM,
chosen by Kathy Fagan for Milkweed Editions

It's Not Magic
by Jon Sands of New York, NY,
chosen by Richard Blanco for Beacon Press

Nervous System
by Rosalie Moffett of Athens, GA,
chosen by Monica Youn for Ecco

FEAR OF DESCRIPTION

FEAR OF

DESCRIPTION

DANIEL

POPPICK

PENGUIN BOOKS

PENGUIN BOOKS
An imprint of Penguin Random House LLC
penguinrandomhouse.com

LIBRARY OF CONGRESS CATALOGING-IN-PUBLICATION DATA
Names: Poppick, Daniel, 1985– author.
Title: Fear of description / Daniel Poppick.
Description: New York : Penguin Books, [2019]
Identifiers: LCCN 2019008206 (print) | LCCN 2019008774 (ebook) | ISBN
    9780525506225 (ebook) | ISBN 9780143134381 (paperback)
Classification: LCC PS3616.O659 (ebook) | LCC PS3616.O659 A6 2019 (print) |
    DDC 811/.6–dc23
LC record available at https://lccn.loc.gov/2019008206

Printed in the United States of America
10 9 8 7 6 5 4 3 2 1

Set in Berthold Walbaum Book Regular

Designed by Elyse Strongin, Neuwirth & Associates

For my parents

Not tied or manacled with joint or limb,

Nor founded on the brittle strength of bones,

Like cumbrous flesh; but in what shape they choose

Dilated or condensed, bright or obscure,

Can execute their aery purposes,

And works of love or enmity fulfill.

−John Milton

They were in the world, and of the world, and their feet laid hold on Hell.

−James Baldwin

Not all that's heard is music.

−Lorine Niedecker

CONTENTS

FEAR OF DESCRIPTION

RED SEA

I'm terrified of a number of fates,
Poisoned water under a tyrant's wage,
Being fired for doing nothing, my parents dying,
Committing a thought like this to the page,
The splash of acid to the face
A Queens nonprofit boss received
Leaving work one blue August evening. Hell's
So eloquent and poetry's no fate at all
Unless you count the story of the divided sea
Waiting to wash its assassins away.
Says the Pharaoh, "That's so sad."
But that story is less fate than news, whereas
That Queens boss? Permanently burned. The *Times*
Says one eye won't stop weeping.

For some months now I've been returning to this one night from late 2016. We were at Kristen's. She had received this jigsaw puzzle as a housewarming gift and had enlisted me and Ariel to help her finish. It wasn't the traditional picture of a waterfall or dew-drenched fawn. In fact there was no figuration at all—just a gradient that swept between a tropic green and a hospital blue. It was a week after she had moved into her new place. I was excited to see the house. She had saved up for almost two decades to buy it. The first home I'd ever entered owned by a friend. Property is the syntax of the reddening horizon. There we were, splashed on just this or that side of thirty, surgically reassembling a color so cool it was really closer to a cry than a hue. She hadn't yet completely unpacked the blank room we sat at the end of, and it was cavernous—a kitchen that bled seamlessly into a living room. What would she hang on the walls, she wondered. A spidery beat lilting from the laptop on the floor. The lamplight looked smaller than it had in her old place—it didn't quite reach all the way to the ceiling. I sipped my Sazerac and felt symphonic, like a smooth, dumb stone over which cool water rolls. I listened intently to the playlist as it flowed by. The music was so cool and I hated it so much, and I noted how sweet it felt to hate cool music; it was the beginning of the end of our youth, a tipping point I've marked at least once a month for the last seven years, and it feels real each time because in fact so far it always is. A siren went by outside. It was November. An enormous pile of books stood teetering against the wall as Kristen's cat batted the blinds. We were making no progress on the puzzle. I love to dance, but I hate games—I love to hate them. These rainy-day exercises people use to be together when they have nothing to say to one another. Why can't we just talk or not talk? Was it even raining? No, the stars were out. The only games I like negate competition. I wonder what I mean by that. "I think a piece is loose—see how it wobbles?" Kristen laid her hands flat on the puzzle and shifted them minutely back and forth, tectonically, and the surface rippled. She took a rip off her tiny bong and passed it to me over the table. She and Ariel have a bond that runs on its own idiom, but we've all three built a harmony of shit-talking these last years that I've come to cherish. We share a sense of premature nostalgia—that a moment always ends too early, a gold thread spun from the straw of what's already happened stitching the future into the present tense. Kristen grew up on a farm in Wisconsin and is the only person I know who seems genuinely energized by living in Brooklyn in 2017. We were neighbors in Iowa City, but we didn't really properly meet until we both moved east. She was designing books and I was working at a bookstore. The first time we hung out I found her on the street in front of the bar where we were meeting, on her phone, yelling at someone about a font. She saw me, smiled, held her finger up, turned around, and continued yelling. Ariel held cardboard shards up to the light to determine the precise shade of blue or green so we could place them accurately inside the lily pad this crooked puzzle was beginning to resemble; then looking more and more, as the evening wore on, like a reflection of selfhood itself–Narcissus staring through the pieces of the pond–a surface soft as planetary id that no one who names himself "one" could love. Were I it, I'd do what it did. Outside, distant music echoed off the street. I squinted and tried to make my eyeballs, awash with pleasure but not industry, articulate the difference between "aqua" and "teal." Even in the moment it seemed like a pretty tidy parable for going insane. But maybe that's the industry of heaven, getting over its wall so your reflection can speak to you directly. At one point I realized we were all staring at our hands. We were in no shape for this game, but we went on. It was November, but what "it" was we could no longer say. The air was getting chill, not quite freezing over, and somewhere to the west of us a wave of rage was washing up on the machinery of the season. Ariel pushed a bright little knob of blue perfectly into its hollow. I paused the playlist I loved to hate and in its stead put on *Rumours*. As "Second Hand News" started up, a cozy silence settled in between us, and a creaturely interruption spilled across the room. We worked for a while and made no progress. Ariel and I have known each other a bit longer. We first met at a Labor Day barbecue about seven years ago in Iowa City, and I asked her about her writing, trying to make small talk. She looked past me over my shoulder, and her face flattened and rescheduled itself into a glyph that said, in the universal language of inward narration, "Now I am dealing with a moron." It's not uncommon for writers to assume you're an idiot if you're friendly. So I didn't attempt conversation with her again for another couple of years. She now claims to have no memory of this interaction, and I have no memory of when we picked up the thread from there, but we gradually followed it into the present tense. She's prone to excessive narrativization, an affliction and a gift. "I love spreading rumors about myself," she said tonight as we walked up her frozen street. Back at Kristen's house, staring into this oceanic jigsaw piece, I wondered how or if my friends would recount this evening to one another at some later date; who would remember things correctly as they happened, and what we would all get wrong; and if we would ever verify it accurately among one another, being our only witnesses, before we slowly melted down to be sipped up by worms, the whole scene as we remembered or forgot it blown away and buried in the architecture of our dust. This is the only game I can get behind: what do you run from in writing? A sentence turns to you in the starlight and stares into you with an amiable cruelty that only art achieves. I'm delaying my point. After what seemed like a long time Kristen cut through the music and said that back home on her family's farm in Wisconsin, something was wrong with the chickens: they had developed a taste for insulation. "A taste for insulation?" I said. Yes. One day in September when her mother opened the latch to feed the chickens as she always did, she noticed that their mood had shifted. They swarmed around with an unprecedented, dark enthusiasm and started pecking at the coop's outer edge. They were going after the pink fluff that lined the structure, the stuff that kept them warm. *Never going back again.* I recognized my life plotted in dim shapes on the other side of the high and naked ceiling. An alien geometry installed itself along the surface of an ink so vast and silent that I remembered a poem I'd never written with it, and pitch-black words streamed through me. It was almost artless. Ariel said, "Are you serious?" Yes,

pink fiberglass leaked
between the warped wooden beams
and they ate it all

DUMPSTER

In the new music
I've discovered nudity.
You don't have to sing
Or spell it out
So much as see
The difference between
The air and the air,
Money, chlorophyll and fear,
A phrase cut with
The nakedness that waking is.
No longer invested
In a poetry of what waking is,
I lace my sentences with sleep.
No poem sings beneath
This sly beat.
The bomb detonates
On a Chelsea street
And your bed is animated
By its laughter
As Saturday enters
A pre-midnight stage.
I can't commit
This sound to the page.

ARIES

1.

Vent your folly, interceptor.

You remind me of a ray.

Motivated in a line that runs into a watery wall.

Waiting for that wave to break, I look at me among the grass

From the shadow of load-bearing beams.

Where a gray cat ruthlessly waits

For his attention, and a lover sleeps.

This cat's outline is clear, I am well suited to watching
        him here

From a rain-slicked skull

Animated by unearthly laughter.

Slamming into a glass that prevents him from his nature.

Purrs, swats at his brother,

And tears at the corner of our bed as I wake from a dream
        he erases.

It's still early in the century.

I think he'd like to eat

And will, and yet by dint of our mutual desire

He and I send death out to earn its wage.

And by this economy of windows, pronouns, damage, and
        Science Diet

Poetry runs into the atmosphere.

Inside the trachea I find a house conveniently protected
        from all interjection.

Rodents crowd the rafters

Packed rigid with crypto-nutmeats

I dare not crack.

And so, writing on June 15, 2016, from an island off the grid

After a year in which I turned from those I love,

Sloughed off my "positions" one by one,

Teacher, bookseller, personal assistant, editor, publicist,

    copywriter, and finally

The throne of content strategy

By which I was to enter economic adulthood,

I find I am only the expression of my actions, not my labor,

My deeds the expression of events,

Events in deprivation so exquisite they require a poet to sing

    their rot.

A zone comes across the forest, the edge

I measure by the shade.

One foot is gray, the next one green.

I walk across the distributive spring

And lower my mouth to the stream.

We feed on song to fend off one another's flesh

Or the terminal phase of a drink

That doubles as a phrase.

What is this *dandelion wine* you say?

I have grown sharp from the harvest,

I cut a song down with my dumb saw.

The quotation marks snapped from the branches

And split open as they hit the ground.

But I somehow sense there is much else among me, much

    else beyond these.

Just saying.

I saw a silent film in April in which on the shore a gramophone
　　turned in a bag of Sunday oxygen.

The day obliged by opening its mouth and letting a drop
　　of nectar exude from its tongue.

The royal lice, as described in Karl von Frisch's
　　The Dancing Bees,

Survive on this standing offer from the queen.

"Being one of those peculiar species that have lost their wings

As a consequence of their parasitic way of life."

And thus a sweetness is not born, but made.

I'm writing a volume on how clover has benefited from
　　the raid.

The people in this environment—imagine if you could see
　　them on

A nocturnal splitscreen emptying its gland into the Roman air.

Everyone in this theater is a stair.

Hating and loving warmth alike, he spiked through the spruce.

I feel my kin most acutely when they are audible or away.

I feel most neutralized in my employment

When the cats have not destroyed my buds

And I employ them.

The music disburdens the branches

And my lean prose bursts into grief.

Pink essay.

It is written in you if you if you

If you if you

Know a person. I know one

Who hails from a most impressive crest.

I no longer recall his exact name.

I preferred the one I called him privately to the one he was
    given at birth.

I believe it was Sweet Charity Greenbreast.

But at this late stage I can scarcely say I have that "in the bag."

Look at me. I feel rag.

My spine draped strangely up.

I speak slowly from it, often with my hands

To cup the vapor exiting its source.

I say.

My breath sounds a little Latinate to me.

Does it to whom?

But in a common way.

2.

Reader, you remind me of a day.

A periwinkle-tinted ozone whipping around until
    entirely gone.

Its winds have blown the line taut. My wit has turned,

My will has bent my laughter to a ring like a spoon

And I am left with strange intelligence. Meanwhile
    the island says

It's true, aesthetic forces do constrict the language.

Is a snake an aesthetic force?

Yes,

But also managed by a despot. Say it with me,

"The snake's quick management curled into its coronation."

And yet that sentence carries less than half an alphabet.

Creaturely notes wriggle up my brainstem, and make
    me laugh.
But I can math.
It banged around in me, rain on the street,
Rain on the roof, rain so famous it fell from the mouth
    of every flower it employed.
I can only describe inhabiting that weather as being
    reconstructed
As my own cerebellum's music.
Slipping from alien stocks into the evening, a deadbolt
    clanking on the pavement,
A mic embedded in its dun corona
To record the angel that is the ground.
It was April when I heard that sound.
I had a flight to catch.
"River, be careful not to get your shoes caught," said
    the woman on the moving walkway
To her running son. And another thing.
A shelf of novels bent off my line of sight,
Perceptible only prior to their sentences, by title:
The Soft Mask,
I Couldn't Remove Myself,
As the Tower Stops,
My Ligature,
The Dancing Worms,
Plays and a Table,
The Sound and the Technological.
Shaken like a box of fresh petals from the stem of your syntax.
You in the plural.

In the plural you agree that color is tantamount to number,
    paint is proxy for the soul,
And the name Ajax is its own scaffold, the kind
On a construction site that gives the building its limit.
As words, a paint of the mouth,
A thin coat applied to the world, and when they meet a wall.
We call this hex "my patience."
I chased it through the garden.
Quick, said the paint, the leaves are full of kids.
I can't afford to befriend Ajax,
"War" or the air around a building,
But words pound further up the gothic stairs every time I talk
    to Alex.
There's nowhere else to charge.
He draws this from me, a negative sun.
In other words a giving one.
I have grown sick on the sunlight, my ride on the sunlight
    was ill.
As at a certain hour an upturned mirror
Is mask for evening.
It's chill.
During evening's first rehearsal I was interested in nothing
    but its costume.
Morning broke and populated it with carnivores and rhyme.
A rhyme lifted its head from a freezing stream.
Rain ran down its antlers.
It met the ice.
My surface senses a creature's approach, pivoting
From a blunted Viking light to the colony's clatter.

I consider the names of some acquaintances who stand deeply
　　up in the full bricolage of that diurnal beat.
The little district of letters more accurate than the human
　　navigators who inhabit it.
I barely know these people, but like Orion sliding
Over alien corn,
They concoct my automatic fiction.
Matt, I hope your consumption flattens.
Keenan, I hope you choose school.
Elisabeth, I hope the otter remains.
Eleanor, I hope you care.
My ligature has bent its lair
In shelves of thawing daffodils, their sagging tongues clean
　　from the just-departed frost.
Richard, I hope your home's surfaces continue to stream.
Bob, I hope your friend's surgery went.
Frankie, I hope you start your slam channel.
The evening is cool and down.
The fire ram rises and rips its enamel.

3.

I met my friend's family on Saturday.
It was Passover.
Hard bread was there to remind us to suffer
And an infant named Liv.
"Liv"—I was hoping this would also be their private nickname
　　for me.
That I could somehow bury it among the roots of their

beflowered brains,

That I would earn their moniker as a nightingale has hers.

As a wave shatters a spruce and in so doing lengthens it

A ripple is the limit of this wish.

I think people ripple

But when they break they don't lengthen. People are inns.

Have you met this shell? It holds my uncle

Until a singer coaxes him out with tidal tone, his antennae
    breaking into the ambulatory air.

Air's technologies can fall in love with one another just

As Narcissus attempts to kiss his double, a phone call flies
    through the night

And slams into a valley.

The foundation of the tragicomic.

I think language, for me, is a tool of differentiation from my
    bloodline

Bound to break down and fail.

Language chooses what to say with you,

It says the waves, reiterated crimes.

While walking on the rocks I was approached by a boat.

The man in it yelled out to me.

I held my hand to my ear.

He cut his engine to make himself more audible.

His hair was gray, his voice a bending reed.

He gestured across the archipelago. *This is my office.*

Nice day for it, I said.

His orange suit arrayed across the water. *I'm gathering snails.*

Then he ignited, rumbled away.

The channel rose in a series of strokes

The way punishment moves through a meadow.

Side to side and vertically, but also just

Around. Collecting injuries and communications as you yank
   at a lilac, its shape

Pushed up flush with the end of things.

A room overruns from me.

Not people, the church in which I sing.

Let us show you to your room.

The king spills into the grass.

The grass spills into the fen.

The fen spills into the flies.

The flies spill into the frog, the frog into its hunt.

Its hunt spills into a snake.

The snake into the lilies.

The lilies spill the pond. The pond spills over the dam.

The dam spills

Into the village. The village spills into a stream.

This stream spills into evening.

Evening builds to midnight

And midnight into the prison.

The prison exits into wire.

The wire spills into a citizen.

The citizen spills alkaline.

Another spills into his phone.

The phone spills into its signal, its signal into space.

Space spills into people.

The collective spills into the park.

The park spills into Saturday.

Saturday into the novel. The book spills over the table.

The table spills up from the floor.

The floor spills over the island.

The island spills into the ocean.

The ocean, installed in the prince.

The way punishment chases information never mirrors

The way information runs away from one's life.

For the first time in my life, on April 3, 2016,

I saw my building as I flew over it.

"As love requires a politics, worldliness cathects."

Truth is difficult because it carries with it the stink

Of its production, like a cat.

A car with spinning rims passed me as I opened my
　　building's door.

I call this smell William.

William digresses from the melting ice.

Will you will it to your will or will you not, William?

Digressions are suspicion

That the prescribed way is false,

Like the open grove where the sun spears its children

And the iris chases heavy metals through the sand.

4.

The instrument is the mirror of the hand.

Lilac pulses along the fence. Perhaps your behavior will be bad

Because you believe language truer than an act.

I think we can see that this is not so,

And by "we" I mean myself.

Have you met my uncle? His name is Rim.

The sweetest nectar gets the briskest traffic.

Like the smell of the donkey by whom you entered.

I feel the sea in my mouth.

A hexagon returning from a far-flung land with news.

It sticks to my tongue.

My tooth has fallen from its meadow

Waiting in the rain on a dock,

Recriminations running through it, or general thought.

Over a number of years you behave in so many ways that in
    the end

No matter what people say of you, they're right.

From this point until the following spring I will wear thought
    in a pendant around my neck.

But what can we say of the neck itself?

A lucent signal without wire.

To be wireless is, I think, to love.

A wireless harbor twinkled under leaden midnight.

I called to it and it responded, but I couldn't hear its reply.

A call that for all I tried would never lift.

I wanted this for it.

As the evening neared and I rolled closer to the centerpiece
    of its event

I encountered a Subaru. It was by then early May.

The trees were greased with swallows.

Its wheels were at rest.

And all around us the bored grove stood

Rapt in its compunction.

A stream wheezed.

I stretched and scratched a tanager.

It purred and sailed away.

Screeching metal carries me closer to the temple of my
  employment.

My bosses must think this a private tour. It is less.

Speed, the music of public transportation.

When I asked what she wanted she just looked at me
  and tugged the sheet.

The gray cat looked at us, conversed, and tore at the corner
  of the mattress.

This intersection of of and and,

A satellite theater of hell.

The voice cut off mid-vowel,

And when I say "the" here I mean "my,"

Dreaming of my social security number falling down
  a numeral

Then quickly rising once again.

I woke to this rotted record.

A lilac shrieked around the evening.

The wind picked. The horizon inscribed

An edge of the property.

It is June 14, 2016.

Tomorrow I will be the precise age my dad was, down to
  the day, when I was born.

I wish to speak to my contemporaries.

Whatever comedy this soft office is, the body inside is
  happily alone.

We have arrived at work.

I see a shepherd standing above my bed with a bucket of ash
hanging from his hand.

He applies his theory to this reader's chest.

Reader, my surface is notorious.

It is dumb, like a quality of rain.

I broke from the building and ran from its front into a staff
of daffodils.

They looked at me and made a claim.

What can I say?

I felt uncommon among them, a little bell.

I was happy and thinly rinsed with fame.

ECSTATIC ZERO

Paradise has a limited vocabulary. Hell is more eloquent,
Letters drop off blackened boughs and splash
Into a stream that feeds down to a fluid realm where poems
Speak for stones. A little ripple spills
Into a honking syllable's bill, green scum snapped up from
The surface of Narcissus's phone. Then it is still.
Interceptor, that face before yours
Locked in a razor-thin, liquid cell
Bears the first fungus: a duplicate life
Whose harmony is not your own.
You open your mouth, and in the water an empty suit
Turns his head, information and defense
Spilling from its pit
In the shitty willow's boundless shadow.

> I set out after composing this verse, the first of my journey, but I could barely keep going ahead, for when I looked back I saw my friends standing in a row, no doubt to watch until we were lost to sight.

–Matsuo Bashō, *The Narrow Road to Oku* (tr. Donald Keene)

I entered my boss's security code and pretended I was lifting a strain from a fugue. His apartment was so smooth and stainless that once when I left a fingerprint, he sang that his surfaces were "in disarray." It was by design. An autonomous sensory meridian response (or ASMR) whisper chamber, but splashed with rare art, long eruptions of natural light, and a socialized security system. He, high on pills, fired me before I saw his ferns. But not before he left an Aeolian window open on his computer through which the breeze blew strange silver, and it chimed. Six weeks later he shattered his shoulder in Paris and, in much pain through veils of vitamin hemlock, decided he didn't need a personal assistant. "This isn't a rational decision–it's an emotional one," he said when he fired me. When we were cleaning out his desk two months earlier we came across this little object wrapped in a blue envelope sealed with Scotch tape. He stared at it for a moment and said it was from his mother, but he didn't want to open it "at the moment." He looked as if his gaze was following a heavy ornamental key as it slid into a drain. I had known him for a day. Around this time I began seeing a therapist to whom I often talked about my employers, dovetailing with an ongoing dialogue about my parents. In April, at the age of sixty-one and after thirty years as a litigator, my dad decided he needed to do something different with the time he had left; adhering to a sense that he should be helping people and in regret, I think, for not applying as a young man when his older brother was deployed to Turkey, he joined the Peace Corps. With our family's blessing he left for a tiny village in the republic of Georgia on April 17, 2015. I don't know what was in my boss's blue envelope, and now I never will. He placed it back in the drawer. He was a sweet man, and despite the unfortunate economy that made me his employee in the first place, I wished him well. This was in late October. The following spring I Googled him and discovered that he was dead. Lately my therapist and I have been talking more about poetry than my dad. I've had this theory for the last thirty seconds or so that the Lisa Frank jumping rainbow dolphin sunset "office supplies" thing from the nineties is actually something other than exactly what it is: to be precise, I think the Lisa Frank craze was "actually" a latent attachment to classical dolphin mythology; just as a dolphin saved a shipwrecked Dionysian poet from drowning in the myth, it carries the prepubescent millennial laborer through a rainbow of mind-numbing math homework. I have this theory because I have no job, and I'm stoned. Shortly after getting fired in January I went to Providence to visit David, who was thinking about shaving his beard and wondered if I would sit with him while he did so. We had been through this before. One of the most magnetic things about David is the way he's able to wink at you by flirting with himself (what the ancient Greeks didn't call "reverse ecstasy"), unafraid of getting those Balthazarian donkey eyes of his a little theatrically greasy when they angle inward. Then he gives them a little flutter. It's like he's always about to be tucked in the night before his bar mitzvah. This tradition: years ago we made a wager that if he could finish an essay that had been killing him for months by midnight on March 26, 2011, I would shave my beard in the public sink at our local Iowa City bar. This wasn't so outrageous, but it had also never been done. "Everyone" was excited. David is naturally competitive and performs well under pressure, so after pounding his head on his desk for another week he managed to win with three minutes to spare. "Boom," he said on the phone. He immediately drove over with his own razors and lotion, and surrounded by a small minion, I did the deed right there in the Fox Head. I hadn't seen my face in five years. The following morning, almost strangers, Callie and I went on our first date—a drive through Iowa countryside. The fields rolled out like a thawed wave. We really barely knew each other at the time beyond singing Hank Williams together on Steve and Ellie's porch one night (drunk, I went inside to get my coat, and when I came back out she'd disappeared), but we had decided to give this outing a whirl. As a precaution we had agreed days before that it would be "cool" if neither of us spoke. When I picked her up she nearly didn't recognize me. "Your chin," she said. The air was clear and choppy, almost syllabic. We drove around and talked all day. The next morning she texted me a photo of a purple crocus. Prose is more alive than itself. All I had to do to find love was reconfigure my face. She came with me to Ohio that summer, where Zach and I drove to an alfalfa field flickering with lightning. He was so happy to hear me count between the bolts that he tackled me to the ground. At this point Zach was not yet sick. A few weeks after Callie and I got together David returned the favor by impersonating me onstage in front of an audience of a hundred people in a sly weekly vaudeville show we collectively ran called Talk Art (he stole my signature geometric sweater), and as Enigma's "Return to Innocence" played over the speakers and our friends cheered, he shaved his own beard into an old brass chalice that he presented to me as a gift later in the evening. I was touched. I hid it in my attic as a talisman. The house on Brown Street was already haunted by a glowing white dog and a family of squirrels who woke us every morning. It was the oldest structure in town, originally a trading post that was apparently a stop on the Underground Railroad, predating the Civil War. We had heard stories of paranormal activity in the house from our two landlords, brothers whose parents had owned it since they were children; one of them swore that one afternoon when he had been painting the living room, he stretched out on the couch for a nap, then shortly thereafter woke to antique sounds. When he looked up, he was in a nineteenth-century saloon with a barkeep and men in holsters and stirrups sitting in a line. Then a car drove by, and the scene went back to the present. This was one guy's haunting, and one can be forgiven for feeling circumspect. Maybe he was having a dream with an edge that bled into waking. This sometimes happens if you sleep in daylight or wet paint. I believe that time can pinch in certain spots. You can map your life onto a meadow creased along a serpentine line knotted with fireflies. No one else to my knowledge had encountered the saloon, at least in recent history. But both brothers and the rest of their siblings had one common interlocutor: through their childhoods all of them had seen a glowing white dog walk serenely through the house. It bore no trace of malevolence–in fact its aura was protective. They swore it was there. Then they didn't see it for decades. It just stopped showing up. They learned in the early aughts that decades earlier two tenants had hired an exorcist to come over and clean. In the language of real estate, I think this is called "flipping it." So no one ever touched David's beard in the bowl. It's probably still there. I grew my own beard back the next week. I wonder what I meant by that. Many poets passed through that house. A few even lived there for a time. Some of us were reading "Imaginary Elegies" and *The Changing Light at Sandover*, "At Night the States" alongside "Lycidas"–we were toying with the idea of conversing with the dead. It occurred to us to have a séance many times over the years, but we didn't work up the nerve to make a Ouija board for a long time, until the last winter we were in town, either in December 2013 or January 2014, I can't remember–it was the lip of the recorded present. We thought this would be fun. It was, but it's difficult to say what actually transpired. Callie and I invited a bunch of poets over, just the handful of people who happened to be in town over winter break. Candace was the master of ceremonies. Sean and Rachel and Margaret and Mere all came, along with a guy I liked but didn't know well, Patrick, who had grown up in town. Candace knew what she was doing and had instructed us not to drink alcohol or caffeine or consume any controlled substance a full day before the event. So we were all sober, a rarity at the time. The house leaked heat, so we were a bit chilly. She had brought sage, candles, and an offering of ruby-red Florida grapefruit for any spirit who wished to enter our drafty chamber. Margaret drew the board. Patrick walked through the house with burning sage to scrub every doorway and window. When he came back downstairs he pulled me aside and said quietly that our office had bad energy—he had taken extra care to ensure that it was clean and hospitable for anyone who wished to enter. I thanked him. As Margaret finished the board, she personalized it, drawing a cat next to YES and a dog near NO. I insisted that we also include a glyph of a wireless signal, a point with waves fanning out—you know the one—to acknowledge the digital tools we the living use to recreate a communicative wavelength whose analog version has been around for as long as people have been haunted. We gathered around the board. We turned the lights out, lit the candles, held hands, threw open the "door," and Candace welcomed anyone who wished to speak with us. Margaret and Mere and I put our fingers on the shuttle, a shot glass. We began asking questions. Our cats usually climb all over everything, but I don't remember them being in the room. We received some static, noisy slapstick responses from elemental clowns (Did you live here? NO ASSFD), and then we decided to call upon the dog. I can't tell you all of this; some of it has slipped into unattended corners of my memory and some of it is certainly gone forever. Let's say the voice coming through the board sharpened. We asked if this was a dog. Our fingers moved the shot glass. [Dog] YES. Everyone lit up a little. Was this the glowing white dog that our landlords had told us about, the one who had visited them when they were children? NO LINK. What color are you? BLACK. This puzzled us. Could there be more than one dog that haunted this place? We asked if it knew the glowing white dog that haunted this place. NO. Is this a boy dog? BOY LINK. Is your name Link? NO. What is your name? AJAX. I hadn't thought of this name since reading *The Iliad* when I was eighteen, the name of one of the physically largest warriors in the Achaean army along with one of the smallest, Big Ajax and Little Ajax. I like the name Ajax for a dog. How did you die? LINK. The signal seemed to be fading; the shuttle kept jerking over the dog picture. Ajax, we know you're a dog. It swept back and forth in the top right corner of the board, almost running entirely off every time. Candace wondered aloud if maybe it wasn't running over [Dog] at all. Maybe it was pointing at Patrick. Indeed, Patrick was sitting at this corner of the board, and now that she mentioned it, he was in the line of fire, as it were, like the voice was reaching out to touch him. She asked Ajax if he wanted to talk to Patrick. YES. Do you know Patrick? YES. Patrick was quiet, completely serene. Do you like Patrick? YES LOVEPATRICK. How did you die? [Dog] LINK. Were you a good dog? NO. Then Patrick spoke. Did you know I thought you were a good dog, and I loved you? NO YES [Dog]. Then the shuttle spun around the board a few times, and the voice disappeared. Patrick walked upstairs. We flipped the lights on. I didn't understand what had happened, but Patrick's composure set me at ease. I was prepared to sort of let it go. We opened beers and started chatting. Ten minutes later Patrick emerged down the stairs. He had been weeping. He told us that when he was growing up, blocks from where we were now, his family owned a dog named Ajax, who had had to be put down after being bitten, through a chain-link fence, by a rabid dog. I get chills telling this even now. We were stunned. None of us who had our fingers on the shuttle even really knew Patrick. We barely knew each other—we all just happened to have the same vacation. We had just clearly spelled out AJAX while he sat motionless, not even close to touching the board. I let the grapefruit Candace had brought as a gift for the dead sit on that table for many weeks. Months later Candace told us that the morning after the séance, Patrick, a lapsed Catholic, went back to mass for the first time in a decade and doused himself with holy water. We didn't have any other séances after that. But there's a coda to this story. I found out years later, from multiple other friends who had spoken to our landlords, that in the story they told the glowing dog I had remembered as being white was actually black. There weren't two dogs haunting the house on Brown Street. Just Ajax. So the new ghost was old in me. Which means, if you follow the timeline, that Ajax had been visiting the house decades before he had been born. Can we prema turely haunt a place before we exist in the flesh, be exorcised, conceived, born, dead, then come home again just to talk to sober poets? It's a convoluted path. It makes me think the soul is a syntax. But in English, thorned syntax is often retrospective, slashed back toward the light source into the sentence's stem. Nearly two years later Callie and I lived in Brooklyn, and all the time I felt like garbage. My mom was living alone north of the city in the house where I grew up, and while she and the rest of us had wholeheartedly encouraged my dad to join the Peace Corps, she was having a rough summer alone. One day

Callie and I were walking with her in a manicured nature preserve and farm owned by the Rockefeller family. We go there frequently. We deviated from our customary route through the woods, and she was agitated. She started muttering and walking quickly ahead of us. Callie and I tried to let her anxiety roll off of us. It was a beautiful autumn day. Shortly thereafter we noticed that she had stopped walking, was staring at something in the curve around the path. A fox was standing there ahead of us, staring back, bright red and drenched in light. Beautifully alert. I turned to my mom. She was crying. I asked her what was wrong. She looked at me but was too terrified to speak, as if she had been turned to stone. I took a step toward the fox and it ran into the woods. We kept walking and found the parking lot moments later, but the afternoon had been ruined for each of us, and for different reasons. I think of that fox often. Around this time David and Charlotte sang "Bohemian Rhapsody" to me while I shaved my beard again, little red hairs wincing in the brown, with one or two grays—now from the sorrowful chamber of my own apartment in an effort to become more employable. My thirty-year-old face stung and bled. Our cats looked terrified by their own boredom, or maybe the other way around. At this point Zach was undergoing chemo. In the middle of the morning in the middle of May in the middle of Ohio in 2007, Andrés and I, driving east post-graduation, almost ran over a little pearl-colored kitten mewing through a gas station. We decided it would be safest to bring her with us. She purred and slept on Andrés's lap. He named her Ishtar. At hour six of our drive to New York we pulled over in traffic to check the engine. An officer approached us. Until I saw his face I thought he was trying to help. The interstate was dense with vehicles and fumes. I told him our car was fine, but asked him if he knew someone who might want a cat. He said, well, he could walk her up into the woods and blow her brains out if we wanted, then drove away slowly and edged into traffic. Every morning our current cats sit by our bedroom window and imitate pigeon sounds in an attempt to lure them close enough to murder. Sometimes it almost works, and a pigeon flies up to the window. The cats crouch, pounce, slam into the glass, and cry. It's definitely funny, but I also find it weirdly moving. The pigeons clatter back to the other side of the alley and leave their feathers winding through the air. A feather, residue of flight and guardian of sleep, really is the edge of another realm. I shaved while being serenaded by David and Char in August, I was hired for the personal assistant gig in October, and now here we are again in January. Time replies. In another week I would be fired. I'm still talking about this business of beards because when David and I exchange them, it means I'm awake to forces running parallel to my will. For example, a haibun is a poetic form in which a prose travelogue occasionally breaks into a little song at the end of a thought, a haiku; if my first day with Callie had been a haibun, then the haiku was that crocus photo, and for all the little epochs I've known David, that haiku has been shaving in public. Verse is more alive than life. "When the honeysuckle blooms so sweet it durn near makes you sick" is from a little song my grandfather used to idly sing when he was happy. I search for it, but its lyrics aren't turning up. I wonder if I got them wrong, if it's "where" instead of "when"–it doesn't sound like it's "about" a time of year. In Providence I offered to sit with David while he did the deed himself (his beard had become antediluvian and gigantic while he was writing his dissertation, completely out of line), but he paused to think about it and this led us to another subject, and another, and the night wore on discursively. We forgot about it. Callie and I had been having problems, and David was a little lonely in Providence, so we were taking a weekend to cheer each other up. Before bed, he introduced me to these videos he watches–people enacting soothing passion plays to help others fall asleep. Have you heard of this? ASMR, in addition to being a "response," has the distinction of being both a feeling and a genre, sort of perpendicular to porn. It's a tingling sensation that gathers in the back of your scalp and trickles through the limbs, brought on by a gossamer-voiced actor (they call themselves ASMRtists) often role-playing an authoritative figure like a doctor or a travel agent, a Viking historian or a masseuse. The ASMRtist explains her intentions clearly and gently, and in so doing telegraphs your own value back to you (as if to say, Hush now, you too are soft and transparent), tinseling her speech with sonic triggers. Dragging crystals through the microphone as if the viewer's hair is one of the conventions of the genre. Diegetic finger-tapping on a can of cucumber-scented spray. Donning silver eye shadow to simulate the coins placed over the eyes of those gentle souls who ferry over to the river's other bank–but bottled, and applied with shimmering precision before the bathroom mirror. A ripple passes under her lids, she blinks slowly, and she whispers into your headphones, "Perhaps you can feel the warmth of my hand on your face," stroking the camera lens, leaning into the microphone, barely exhaling: "We tooth fairies are part of a union," and your spine turns to powder. It doesn't affect everyone, but based on my own experience, it seems to induce a momentary synesthesia of touch and sound, like a bat's voice massaging the skull. The object is for sleep itself to become the poem–the ASMRtist is just your Virgil, and tapping not a rhythm so much as a chisel used to correct hell's natural amphitheater, like how at the end of the day I felt engraved on my boss's wall. It's also ecstatic ("reverse ecstasy," what the Greeks never called it). The video David showed me first was by an actor who called her free service ASMRrequests. She played several characters, but her affect was always deathless glass. I wonder what she meant by that. I felt like I could travel in it. David spent hours explaining how it worked, and I was rapt. We were up until three a.m. He didn't end up shaving that night. I could tell he felt superstitious about it–maybe he forced himself to forget. It's nearly impossible to give up the variation of the good life you know best when it's already there: a beard, a pair of shoes, a lover, a horse in the proverbial midstream region (but in so doing, am I giving up safe passage or just my relation to the river?)–it's why I have to touch a certain wall whenever I think of someone I know dying. Well, anyway, the Elizabethans called it dying, but that was before the planet was warming. I went to the Metropolitan Museum of Art to see *Salome with the Head of Saint John the Baptist*, by Andrea Solario. The centers of her pale blue cheeks are flushed as she beholds his green head bleeding from its stem, his ginger hair gathered brutally in some unseen interlocutor's fist, floating above a silver dish she uses to gather the nectar. So this mute tulip hangs, and her gaze, in its devastating sympathy, perched like a feather on the edge of contempt's windswept bluff, is almost his. I went to the museum that day playing hooky from work, because I thought I would lose it if I didn't temporarily escape. Another painting I saw was *Teasing a Sleeping Girl,* by Gaspare Traversi, which depicts a crowd of leering pranksters gathered around a girl napping in the candlelit dark with a box of keepsakes on her lap, an old man dangling a feather over her eye, the sentinels barely holding their shit together. Feathers are a form of torture for the ticklish, and for cats crammed into too small an apartment. In Elena Ferrante's first Neapolitan novel, Lila resists the gleaming new apartment her bougie fiancé likes, the one with "a bidet, and a view of Vesuvius," for a place in an older building with bad light. At the end of the paragraph she gives in, and it takes her a sad half century to disappear. I suppose, then, this is about the places you don't go to live. My grandfather's Houston high-rise apartment has excellent light. In January 2017, just after his ninety-ninth birthday, he tried to eat his hearing aid, and for the first time forgot my name. He asked me to read him one of my poems, so I did. When I finished, he said, "Well, you've lost me there." I laughed and suggested he might like something older, and he agreed. I read him Keats's "To Autumn." When I finished, he said, "Well, you've lost me there." This time I really laughed. My mom turned to me and said, "Do you see how hard this is for me?" We went to see the Cy Twombly painting *Untitled (Say Goodbye, Catullus, to the Shores of Asia Minor)* whenever we visited him. Twombly's script is bruised into the frame, a talking wave washing up on the prismatic shore you are on by virtue of being with it in the room. A yellow muted and thrown off the wall, lit up by a hint of rust that by prescient architectural design phosphoresces slightly when the sun is out even though the painting is indoors. A sign said, NO PHOTOGRAPHY. Still, I caught a picture of my mom facing it, in which color, crushed into a narrow rivulet on the left wall, spills out to greet her. I love this photo. She stares at the scrawled letters O R P H E U S across the gallery as the guard steps through a door to the outer lobby, in the very back of the frame, his hand extended toward me in a feeble attempt to block the lens from duplicating what we saw. The following September I went to see a performance of Bach's *Goldberg Variations.* About a third of the way through, to my shock, I began weeping. It happened so suddenly that my eyes were flooding over before I realized what was happening. It was as if the music had entered a passcode into my face without my knowledge. Sitting in the dark theater, I understood, as if in the logic of a dream, that I was grieving for my grandfather. When the performance ended I checked my phone, certain that there would be a message from my mom telling me that he had died. But there was no such message. Then three months later, in December, exactly one month short of his hundredth birthday, he was gone. Two years earlier, in January 2015, I dreamt Jess was leading me through the Frick after it had closed. We were chatting and walking through the dark and empty galleries, you couldn't see *The Education of the Virgin* or the Turners, and as we rounded the stairwell out of the corner of the eye I saw another friend of ours at the end of the room, and in that instant this person walked into the wall—she went through the wall. And I knew she was streaming around there, in the walls. What else happened before and after that day? Thirteen months prior to that, in December 2014, I wept openly in a court of law when another friend was released on his own recognizance for resisting arrest and allegedly assaulting an officer. It had been on the evening news. Cops had come to get a look at him. They lined the room like rusty lawn furniture lines a basement in the winter. In the middle of the night in the middle of March in the middle of Kansas in 2006, Andrés and I were pulled over for speeding. Andrés was behind the wheel, and the only ID he had on him was his Mexican license. I was pretty sure I knew what happened to people in this situation in Kansas. I was terrified. After the long amble back to the car the cop let us go with a friendly warning and told us to drive safe. We laughed and joked that the guy probably couldn't even read Spanish. Never mind that I couldn't read Spanish either, nor can I now. Ten minutes later, humming through the dark, a tumbleweed blew through the headlights and Andrés, thinking it a live animal, swerved hard, and the car spun across the blank freeway. I saw a deep embankment spinning up to the headlights. It was out of our hands. Four months after the courtroom I was running through Los Angeles late at night to cross an intersection before the blinking man turned red again, and in my third bound came down hard on my rogue right ankle. It twisted and popped. I tumbled into a gutter. I picked myself up off the deserted street and limped away. The walk in the dark back to the hotel was almost Orphic pain. When I got into bed I started shaking, then stopped, and fell asleep. The next morning my dad sent us an email saying he had twisted and broken his ankle and he was quitting the Peace Corps. The synchronicity deeply chilled me. Then that evening I found out it was an April Fools' joke. I wonder what he meant by that. Exactly one year earlier, on April 1, 2015, I was sitting in the public restroom at the Annex taking a shit when the doorknob started to rattle. My polite protest quickly gathered urgency until finally a woman ripped the door out of its lock. She paused for several intervals as we stared at each other, then slowly closed the door. It was the beginning of National Poetry Month. When I exited and smiled—as if to say, This happens, all the time even, and I wish it hadn't, but c'est la guerre, have a nice day despite what we've just done—she wouldn't make eye contact. When I was working at the bookstore a distracted man once forgot to make eye contact with me at the register when I was ringing him up, and inserted his credit card between my fingers as if they were magnetic scanners. It was lodged there for a few seconds until he looked up, realized his error, and half-heartedly apologized. These are the two most New York interactions I've ever experienced. There was a nasty balm of paranoia hanging over the city at this time. That August I read about an incident in *The New York Times* that I've never been able to shake. The executive director of an arts nonprofit in Queens tasked with bringing the sick and elderly to Broadway shows and the opera had been attacked with a cup of lye to her face when she was getting into her car after leaving work. Earlier that week she had discovered that the organization's bookkeeper had been embezzling hundreds of thousands of dollars; this bookkeeper, sensing she had been found out, hired a man to disfigure her boss to shut her up. The bookkeeper and assailant went to jail, the boss continued the organization's good work from her bed in a hospital burn unit, and then the entire organization shut down. It was horrific. A year and a month later, a bomb exploded in a dumpster in Chelsea—several other devices found nearby and at a train station in New Jersey failed to detonate. The city went about its business like nothing had happened; no one here has time to fear for their lives unless they're already dead. I've found over the years that New York's beauty is in direct relation to its wretchedness—the city creates problems that it then solves luxuriously, if you can afford the rent. In March Chris and I went to Kathleen's thirtieth birthday party at the Call Box Lounge. Emile and Elaine and Kendall were there, and I danced with a very sweaty Jake, who looked like a wet sequoia. Emile assured Kathleen that even though it was her birthday, there would be no "hanging out" for her unless she wished for it. "Hanging out" is this "dance move" Emile "invented," where we all pick a friend off the ground and hold them in the air, chanting "Who's hanging out? She's/He's hanging out," before putting that person back on the floor and continuing to actually dance. It mostly comes up at the parties he and Allie throw at their apartment every year the week before Thanksgiving, but we're getting older and the practice is waning; Kathleen thanked him, and said that tonight she would prefer not to hang out. This was the primary conversation I witnessed. Robyn's "Dancing on My Own" does things to me that I don't want to understand. After the party, in the hours just before dawn when Chris and I were walking wearily through my neighborhood looking for food, he told me a story. At the party he had spotted, across the room, a brilliant writer whose books he adored. He gathered his nerve and approached her in the space adjacent to the lasers and mirror ball, and through waves of bass and synthy Bieber told her he really loved her writing. She seemed skeptical of this visage at first, smiling poet-scholar blinking in the non-ironic discotheque, but she came around and they began to have a real conversation. By his account, this is what happened next: she was in the middle of saying something to him when suddenly his brain couldn't handle the fact that he was talking to this person, he was too starstruck—and it reset. A creaturely interruption overtook him. And in that instant he forgot that she was talking to no one but him. She was in the middle of her sentence when he blurted, "Hi, I'm Chris!" He heard himself say this and realized his error exactly as the words left his mouth. A cool horror washed over him. She stared at him for a moment and said, "Yes, I know—we've been having a conversation." I can't tell you how much I love this story. But this isn't about those incidents; it's about the melting of the present tense. I said goodbye to Char and David, and on the way home from Providence, still haunted by David's lecture on ASMR, I visited an estranged relation for the first time in over a decade. She'd always been nice to me and my brother and sister when we were kids. She seemed happy but unnerved to be there. We talked about her dogs. "Good to see you—I really mean that," she said as we parted, and if it wasn't true she clearly wanted it to be. But I think it was. And I genuinely agreed. I think she thought the future might one day obviate that fate. I for one believe that persons are so miraculous that force can pass between them like detergent enters a shirt. We embraced in the rain. It pattered on our coats and a tingle tranced through me, roving from the back of my head down through my limbs. It was January. It occurred to me later while I was driving home through the rain and singing into the windshield that while I had always known her as an adult, she had only really known me when I was a child. When she sat down across from me she was essentially meeting a second person. This had been harder for her than it had been for me. We're a shifty tribe and our union is a conviction that good intentions descend like snow, which was especially moving that afternoon, as all signs indicated that snow would never fall again. I drove home to those shitty little New York trees bursting into grief—zombie-pink petals had been budding and falling all December. Even the contemporary westerns of that holiday season starred elegiac blizzards and blood: *The Hateful Eight*, *The Revenant*, the last duel scene of the first new *Star Wars*, where they throw lightsabers through a snowy wood and the alien land is dividing under them. I thought this then as one does in rain, but that was a long time, now, ago. Just after midnight on January 28, 2016, David texted me a photo of his clean-shaven face over a caption, "Back to the future." At this point Zach had undergone both chemo and surgery, but they missed a cell or two, and unbeknownst to everyone, a new mass was already duplicating itself just under the skin, inside the surgical scar ("a victory for bad metaphor," Hilary called it when she shared the awful news in an email on July 4, 2016). Tonight on the phone Zach told me that his next surgery, scheduled for a couple of weeks from now, will require a painful skin graft—or, as he put it, "a turducken of pig dick and butt skin sewn onto my abdomen." I love it when he rhymes with himself. The surgery was successful, and he didn't even need the turducken. A year after that I walked past my deceased boss's old apartment and looked at his buzzer–his initials were still there; puzzled, I Googled him again that night. As it turned out, another man from Manhattan–the same age, with the same name and profession–had in fact died earlier that year, but my boss was ostensibly still alive. By alchemic code or grace or another's ear we make our way, flush with the end of things. I'm on an island now. I like being on water, the lip of the country, to see what passes for will and what the world, what objects float up to me and decay in the sun. At midnight in the middle of January 2009 Andrés and I walked out on the frozen pond in Prospect Park. We didn't talk. It was dark, and at some distance we saw an object half-embedded in the ice. We approached it. It was a pineapple. I kicked at it gently, knelt down, and pried it out. Andrés and I weren't doing very well. I hated my job, and every morning for two full hours I wrote poems about colony collapse disorder on personalized stationery the company had provided, telling my employers when they passed my cubicle that I was "making my agenda for the day." Andrés was trying to get into graduate school and leave New York. It was too hard; he didn't have a job, and his brother, Juan, our roommate, was surviving on cans of tuna fish. Our house was infested with mice; we had a giant poster of Hieronymus Bosch's *The Garden of Earthly Delights* that for some reason had a giant nail bursting out of the wall from behind it, ripping a hole through its center. I think we did this on purpose to make it look "genuine." We were sick of each other. It was a work night. We spread out over the pond, and with heavy metals frozen under our feet we kicked the skittering pineapple back and forth across the logical ice, A to B and back again. As for Juan, he died this June. I'll get to that some other time. In any case, I spoke too soon about snow: five days before David sent me that text about his beard and the future, New York had been buried under a historic drift. Callie and I pushed our way out of our building to see it from the inside. The wave that was the landscape washing up on our first date had reared back and frozen again. It had been a hard few months for us, but that night we were happy. Every square inch of air was white, and in the park the dogs were all autonomous. Their owners were yelling for them in the distance. A shepherd mix emerged from the static, smelled our hands, ran past us, then mere moments later came back from the same direction like we had been spliced into the evening's previous reel. I have a photo on my phone from that night of Callie with a huge smile plastered over her face while she watched another dog as it jumped and buried its head in the snow outside the frame, big flakes drifting around her. An ambulance drove by, its siren smothered in a polar fur. Floodlights angled up at the Prison Ship Martyrs Monument, and in them you could see discrete pieces fall. A row of parked cars flowed into a single structure in the wind, every curve and angle suggesting alien aircraft or contemporary design: all snow that falls in the present tense these days is monumental for time we don't have–that's why being in it feels sci-fi. And it fell. Across the river my boss slept it off. Under lit windows people were sledding down their stoops. At first and even second glance the underworld is deeply moving, but I've never looked more than twice. I wish I could play that shadow like a lyre and whisper its slumber back to you. I'm not changing the subject, nor could I if I wanted to. This is my elegy. For a time we shared it, and in the end we could not agree upon all of its events, so I say goodbye in the blizzard. Today I found a piece of porcelain in the water. I looked up at the flat sea and the glare burned my eyes. "Oh, so it's twin language," my therapist said of poetry. When I left my boss's apartment for the final time I locked the door behind me, and from the other side the space sang, YOUR SYSTEM IS ARMED. I hope you also have

a blank space between
your head and feather pillow
that's automatic

HELL

Is a solar refusal
Whose cry is its description. Buildings
Evade their engineers
As they scale the streets,
As I evade the author of the apple or
An apple ascends the hot horizon
Flush against an alien breeze,
An earthy urgency laced through the rays.
My grandfather nods at the air he's conditioned
And lovingly eats his hearing aid.
The quick red fox rots
Into the floor; it rots in rhyme.
But this floor is, like . . . glass.
I heard something above it. That music felt fast.

An agile stone flew up to my window.
My voice broke through
Spilling an ancient insecticide
Buried in the architecture of its juice.
The grass's laughter
Hurts him. It hurts me too.
He didn't see me until I kissed his head,
Then smiled and closed his eyes.
Tears such as poets weep freeze
And flutter down on heaven's wall.
This snow falls out of order, splits

The April blossom. Its two halves fly,
Its *in the new music* and *I've.*
That music fell fast. I have to choose.

A happy marriage of seed and design
Feeding its metropolitan worm,
The millisecond chewing through its sister
Hour's toxic flesh. I too refuse.
I kissed his head, he closed his eyes.
Little words drone through asphodel,
Then drop to dry their wings.
That music felt fast. What I hid in it
Ripped from my hide,
Pink petals singing yes to no
And all the dumb sun loses.
The light is flat, my bloodline laughing in it
As they gather on the paving stones.
Vent in the song, I have to choose.

THE ART BUYER

1.

Hurtful and contemporary, I was trying to speak
Directly in May.
The snow melts,
We smoke on fire escapes, TROILUS AND CRESSIDA
    and THE TAMING OF THE SHREW
Splashed across city buses all spring, buds dun and then
From instant to instant
They flood and burst, and purple psychosis blooms across
    the surface
Of the city. And then comes June.
An unknown number called me twice before I picked up
    on the third attempt.
Mythology is this feeling that comes to you near streams.
It was not mythology but sorrow
That was artifice's original affect. Sorrow is a rune.
One's techniques fan out across the evening to talk
But conversation is a tune in the heat.
My phone said Juan had entered the falls.
Techniques as it turns out only take instructions
From their parents on up, but death moves in a ring.
Today is the first day of summer.
I felt happy by this stream and the next,
I think they must be animated by one who animates the week,
Water animating stones and denizens.

So water is parental: strong, cruel,

A cell with openings and shops,

Butchers, grocers and monuments,

Come solstice we gather by a pool of it

To celebrate gravity's reset

And the body of the king we live inside is stuffed with straw

To burn collectively.

The sea had a footlight on its edge named Satan,

Satan is a sail

Who catches the western wind and crashes through its wall.

I'm delaying getting to my point.

Three days ago Andrés's brother Juan, with whom I haven't
    spoken in years,

Slipped on a rock in Las Nubes, Chiapas,

Fell into a surging current

That sucked him under

And went down a waterfall he'd been painting.

They recovered his body yesterday.

A mass will be held in San Cristóbal on Thursday.

They found his painting resting on another rock, water
    running around it.

When I heard I walked into the woods and wept,

But let's admit it: while the tears were real

"Wept" is not the word for what I did,

And when he and I were both alive my love for him was cut
    with a thought

That he was arrogant and dramatic, way too pure.

He wouldn't let people cook for him but stole food when he
    was alone.

We lived in a mouse-infested house off Nostrand
And when he saw one shattered on the kitchen floor,
Its back snapped,
He screamed, walked back to his room, and slammed
  the door.
Once he saw my dad in a shirt that read LIFE IS SIMPLE
EAT FISH, and fell mute, fuming.
He made huge, expensive scans of his paintings when he was
  too broke to buy groceries
And tried to put them up in the New York museums.
Once in Paris he stripped in broad daylight and jumped into
  the Seine
To swim across and impress a girl, but the current started
  dragging him under
And the police picked him up in a boat. Dumb little Prospero.
Andrés's reverence for his antics was total, he hung on
  every word,
And I hated them both for it. But it was obvious
Juan was possessed by genuine fire. His pictures
Dark and slashy, vatic and profane. A delicately sinister
  beauty radiated from his lips.
A week after he fell
His mom posted a photo of the final painting he left on the rock.
He'd given the falls an alien agility,
Like they were hovering just above the canvas,
And his palette had lightened since he'd moved home, a thin
  lilac net on the upper edge,
Blues and greens.
It was brutal. I stared at the painting on my computer at work

A week after our parent company fired the art buyer for

No reason. I remembered in that moment how he'd hex me
    in Spanish to Andrés,

Steal my lentil soup, and one night gently insisted, after I said
    it looked dumb,

I was wrong, *Singin' in the Rain* was sacred.

In any case

My theories about his freedom are over. I only know he was it,

A raining book

Who theorized himself by accidental communication.

I call this book

He, another one with a narrative,

Because he is too much in motion to avoid the lie, when
    in reality

The entirety of night reaches toward this afternoon

And cinema sings behind the curtain of Juan

While he mouths the words he memorized

In silence. The stone he decorated with the price of
    his materials,

The celestial breeze and ripped horizon, monotone boats,

And almost successfully regulated lust for falling water

Genuflecting to the phosphorescent particles blinking on
    its surface

As dusk turns and laughs.

I am with this laughter as a port

Receives its daily rage.

Rage is in season. It is nearly September.

The sun entered my skin and grief beat through its theater.

I'm playing on two screens.

I've been reading about colonies and communications.

"The watchful keeper will rid her of her unwanted guests

By blowing smoke at her

While holding her in the hollow of his hand,"

Says Karl von Frisch in *The Dancing Bees* of removing lice

    from the queen.

One of those was right that said language can ripen to a

    terrible autumn.

"And this is the meaning of the 'Battle of the Drones':

Not a sudden upsurge, or a 'Massacre of St. Bartholomew',

    as some

Poets, writing of bees, would have it;

But a slowly rising hostility on the part of the worker-bees

    which may drag on for weeks,

Getting fiercer and fiercer

All the time, until every single drone has been killed."

People are awful and poets are tyrants, but who said

Tyrants are not poets. Says the tyrant,

"That's so sad."

I think punishment is evidence of someone else.

The purple iris that drops its root in sand doles out

    a punishment self-justified.

Poetry has done its work on you

Insofar as you are with people and flowers

But your love for its glyphs looks thin from the balcony.

And in Satan's argument over the sea the odor of the

    prideful iris

Lends it accuracy; an iris drifted over the pit

And we saw the pit was true.

The air was so still I heard voices coming in from
the mainland.

A loon buried in red glare.

Rotted light and wind can overfill the vein. Wind can take it
out of you

Like sentences, light can take the contagion

Out, so the wound rolls through.

It might earn its passage out as Ariel earns theirs,

And thus we come to the coast.

I will lie prone in it

As a crab crosses my spine, the cool water lapping up on my
burnt back.

I the tide's tool, the tide

Mine. Ariel begs the tide

To plant its eyes in my chest, waits for the charge

And clear.

2.

Seawater trapped in the ear

Drips onto this indolent paper. Occasionally

It is inflected with a dye that briefly turns the bonfire green.

Autumn is the season of economy. It is upon us early

In the form of an election, so I have not escaped the other
infection

Tumbling through the middle air.

The spruce are full of a magnetic, martial song.

It is this and less, a concert of recorders

Like the faces of my best students, one of whom today
    admitted

She often came to our class stoned.

I love being prone on the flood. But have you ever been prone
    on the flood

On weed? "While night

Invests the sea." I love that break.

I used to teach, but now I work "in start-up tech"

And I'm trying to turn back.

The company I work for just fired half of everyone for
    doing nothing,

They even fired the art buyer

And that's why the company exists, to sell drones, earrings,
    and sex toys alongside paintings,

But so far no one's fired me.

Perhaps these flowers of malignant fantasy, their flames
    fanned by art,

Correspond not by coincidence

To the decor of the actual world, which I take great pains not
    to call "the real."

A cloud of one rains on the other

And by this grace the meadow arrives, I mean flowers are
    the costume

Of the real. I follow the irises down to the water.

They break the port down to each item, petal by petal away—

Here is the prow, here the wheel,

Here the box of stemware that must be messaged from its
    straw, here the glass

Looking at the new land, here is the oyster,

Here the rat, this inch of rope,

A distance with a bolt flickering at its rim,

Here is the cake, the name written on it,

The hospital on the hill and the cell that steals you to it,

The undiscovered strain of influenza tumbling on the breeze
   toward shore.

I'm being indirect, which I'm prone to when I'm reading.

"He wasn't interested in limits," Andrés said on the phone
   the other night.

Night is a limit. Is the line?

What makes Satan pathetic as he glides along the water is

He doesn't realize he's

A tool.

Unless over his own cool depths

He tools,

And this he knows well, the verb,

Thus the tyranny of heaven ripples and bends with
   one's arrival.

Only in hell or art

Can the phrase "the flower of heaven"

Vibrate through our Roman air.

Today is the first day of summer.

I watched the longest sun of the year go down from a boat
   in the reach.

People were snapping photos as it dropped beneath
   the clouds.

The first question Juan asked me when I met him was,

If I knew the world were ending, would I write poetry?

When I answered, he saw something in me I don't know.

A glittering cruelty played its scales between us.

The Halloween we lived together

He dressed as Andy Warhol in an old black suit, baby powder
in his hair.

We threw a party, and he hid behind a camera and filmed our
friends for several hours.

When we carried Andrés up to bed, Juan recorded it.

While we were chanting for Andrés to look alive and Andrés
puked, Juan recorded it.

Andrés slept and he filmed, transfixed.

To be transfixed is to be stuck on an arrow

Not oneself, not of one's world,

Obscure clover, the *bienenwolf wespe* and royal lice.

"One can still fill whole books with descriptions of
their enemies.

In fact there is a wide choice of such books. But in the present

One we shall mention only those which are of particular
importance, and,

At the same time,

Have rather fascinating qualities."

That's Karl von Frisch on bees again. The angel of speech

Tangled in my idiotic net.

Poetry infected me on a summer day, far before the leaves of
hell began to fall.

"Let none admire that riches grow in hell."

Let none admire a meteor,

Or an exhalation emptying from its temple to become a tone

In the fugitive air, filling the ear

Where it wrecks. When we exit this poem (when we escape)
We will have endured a period of deprivation. Thus we earn
Our passage out, having made our deposit.
An unhappy language in a happy word.
Let none admire the direction of my speech. It is only as
    brutal as its source.
"Oh, so it's twin language," my therapist said of poetry.
In his final email to me on December 11, 2015, Juan wrote,
"Dear D., I hope you are doing well. My life is a wreck.
I've had no girlfriend since we last saw each other. That is
    the saddest thing I could say.
I wonder what 2039 will bring.
Could you please recommend this article of mine to any
    literary magazine?
Any option is fine by me. It is about how Shakespeare wrote
    his Sonnets
In memory of his dead son. It could be a ground-breaking
    piece,
But all my attempts at publishing it have failed.
Come down to Mexico as soon and for as long as you can."
The final line of the essay he attached reads,
"The dedication is, in fact, an epitaph, a message inscribed
    onto a tomb:"
I decided then not to have the time for these theatrics
And never replied.
Karl von Frisch: "This is all the more remarkable, as the bees
    do not carry watches.
The bees have no word for 'up' in their language.
There are no flowers in the clouds."

Words go dark because they're comorbid with rain,

A rain that collected, gathered force

And spoke him back. And if I'd received them?

"He looked bigger, and I finally understood that line

'Those are pearls that were his eyes,'" Andrés said on

    the phone.

I didn't know what to say. I tasted the work of his sentence

Like a drone tastes its planet's syntax, nectar

Blown across a glasslike sea.

Ariel remains or flies away.

In any case

They leave their shield.

FEAR OF DESCRIPTION

Fluid curse

Cut loose from the face

Aeolian window

Singing my costume

The rain too wrongly falling to run in

When asked in an interview

Do I want the position

By night I do

No by day

And mute life plays, rising to the skin

To dream this concrete

Shape we're in

THE HELL TEST (SEVEN SPRINGS)

1.

In the new music I've discovered nudity. Idiomatic footfall marking its route over a pane of glass, plunging into a darkened meadow. An interruption in the field filled with a vaporous microphone, titling the air with what it records—an animal running through the grass, stalking the glass, stepping onto it, lowering his snout, and whimpering as he smells the window under his feet.

2.

I used to trespass regularly on a piece of property two towns over from where I grew up. Property is the syntax of the reddening horizon. But "property" isn't the precise word. It was an estate, meadows and mansions, little monuments of infrastructure dotted along its outer edges: an abandoned stable, a shattered greenhouse, a rotting pump overgrown with flowering vines, an enormous house with a fountain in its garden, a pile of rubble, a swimming pool lined with marble. It was decadently abandoned. I told my parents about it at dinner. Alarmed, they told me not to go back, so I did as often as I could. I walked alone there, stoned at the end of my teens, meticulously surveilling myself for signs of profundity that no one credited me; if I could not articulate what I was, I would let the properties on which I trespassed speak for me. Was I *of* this ruined estate?

The place looked like a horror movie even in broad daylight. I always stopped by a spot in the middle of a field, no building in sight, in which a skylight jutted out of the grass over what appeared to be a dank cellar below. There was a hatch a few feet away that I could have easily opened, but something stopped me. I listened for hours on end to music featuring psychedelic mandolin solos and lyrics about talking coyotes, played the role of Dan in an edgeless theater for an audience, such as it was, of one, and was, to what I think of as my present self, insufferable. I was magnetized to suburban ruins, especially if the ruins were under construction, as the knowledge that I was standing in the skeletal infrastructure of what might someday be some unknown family's home filled me with a sharp longing that I loved because it would never be satisfied; I would never be able to gather enough of the multitudinous downed branches of adolescence to build the theater-in-the-round that I imagined adulthood to be. For instance, it was impossible to imagine owning a house. One day, walking through the woods of the estate alone, I felt a presence in the trees off to my left. I looked up and saw, fifty paces through the forest, a structure so large and ominous that the mere outline of it made my blood run cold. I'd never felt that way about a building. A stone tower with nothing around it. I stepped back, then stepped forward. It was January, and along its rim ice seemed to bubble from the ground. I walked up to it and marveled at how close it had been without my noticing. I craned my neck and saw a tree growing on top of it. I had been raised as a Reform Jew—in other words, an agnostic worshipper of narrative—which meant that this image appealed. I wanted to see it up close. I pried open the door to the tower and found a metal water silo inside, corroded and percussively dripping. In a helix around it a rusted set of stairs spiraled up. I tested the first one, and it seemed sturdy enough to hold my weight. I started walking up, slowly, wondering if I could find a latch in the ceiling to get to the top in the dark. Twenty feet up I heard a wet crunch. The stair snapped under me and clattered into darkness–I grabbed the rail, and the entire staircase swung free from its bolt. I caught myself between the tank and stone exterior, and slowly slid myself down, the mechanism clanking in on itself, my heart pounding, the back of my sweater torn up as I shimmied down. I looked down into the dark below my feet and shook. I hadn't told anyone where I was, drunk on solitude and trying to thwart my parents. Had I fallen, broken a leg, been paralyzed, no one would have found me. I drove home and told no one what had happened. Later I heard a rumor from my hometown friends that the property was owned by Donald Trump. In 2009 I confirmed this when I saw the property on the news. The estate was called Seven Springs. Trump had purchased it in the mid-nineties so his sons could learn the art of the deal there, mowing massive lawns to win his love. He wanted to turn it into a golf course that would have poisoned New York City drinking water in an adjacent reservoir, but local government shut him down. It was on the news in that moment because he had rented it out to Muammar Gaddafi for the weekend. I returned and continued walking through the property regularly through my twenties. No one ever stopped me, but I never entered the water tower again. One day I plucked a discarded light switch from a pile of rubble. It's on the shelf behind me as

I write this, wiring exposed in the back, plugged into the air, no wall to take its charge. For years I've wondered if any footage exists of me walking around there. Had I stumbled into a panoptic wood rigged with cameras? But this seems too pristine a nightmare—too fragile and idiotically prophetic, the way a teen is—to be true. What would they have recorded? I wake in the middle of the night sometimes attempting to remember if or how I've broken any other laws, any reason anyone might have to hunt my friends or family, or hold my paycheck. I go to the window to look at the stars and wonder if we could ever live elsewhere. So the new regime is old in me. Beyond the present there is no place, so far as I can tell, where we can go to spend, be robbed, or pay.

3.

In October 2016 Chris and I walked out on a glitzy lakefront in northern Michigan to catch the autumn sun's swoll geometry before the evening events. We were rooming in finished basement bedrooms in the woods that weekend, generously put up by local empty nesters Jim and Laurie for a book festival in the town of Harbor Springs, co-organized by my friend from college, Katie. Chris's car had broken down. The plan had been to head out from Brooklyn via Niagara Falls on Thursday and leave on Sunday afternoon, drive through the night, and return to our jobs early Monday morning with an extra cup of coffee to power us through our exhausted workday; in retrospect I realize that our designs were bent toward a particular variation of failure that thwarts one kind of labor for another. On our way out, just over the Canadian border past Niagara Falls, we found that the car would not accelerate past forty-five miles per hour. Reasoning that we were halfway there and this was fast enough to get us to our destination before Friday morning, when the festival started, we decided to press on. When we arrived a mechanic informed us that one of the exhaust pipes was completely clogged with soot and we were lucky the car had not caught fire while we were driving; there was no way we were getting back on the road until a new catalytic converter arrived from Detroit. It would be nine days. We walked to the coffee shop wearing the only black jeans in Harbor Springs, feeling like we were watching the scene from some bewitched movie theater far away. No question: we were fucking idiots. At the coffee shop we smiled at a woman's beagle as it wagged its tail and sniffed our shoes, and the woman looked at us and asked where we were from. Chris said we had driven in from Brooklyn the previous night, and we would probably be staying for a spell. She smiled and said she'd heard Brooklyn had a wonderful literary culture, and then, looking down at her happy beagle, "We love dogs here. Do you guys have"–darting her eyes back and forth between us–"dogs?" Now we were walking by the lake, a chill cutting through our coats, doing Michigan accents, skipping stones, discussing what new jobs we might apply for, as it was now inconceivable that we wouldn't be fired from our current positions. I took a photo of Chris's silhouette cut out of the lake's blinding glare, yawning deeply in a knit hat, some bright red autumn berries choking their way out of the branches above him. We sat under this tree, sun in our faces, and he patiently let me read him a new long poem I'd written a few months prior, "The Art Buyer," just after Juan had fallen to his death in a waterfall in Las Nubes, Chiapas. We joked that we would probably die on Lake Michigan, covered in the blossom's labor, nothing to show for ourselves but a few loose scraps of "experimental" poetry lodged in a lakeside dune and a broken Subaru back in town. We walked back past waterfront mansions wrapped in plastic sheets to protect them from the brutal winter. Jim and Laurie later told us over a bottle of wine that evening that we were lucky no one had chased us away with a gun—we had been trespassing on a private beach owned by some of the wealthiest families in the state. It was difficult, somehow, to imagine such nice people opening fire on us—but we conceded that we might have been filmed.

4,

I came to a point at which I could only be persuaded that the most ornately phrased facts were true. Blessed with a tuneful voice, I painted, by livid numbers, my parents, my employers, the state. "Oh, so it's twin language," my therapist said of poetry. Fuming in an overstuffed chair, I rolled up my sleeves. But I was so furious for such nonspecific reasons that I couldn't speak. "You seem angry. Can you talk about that?" It occurred to me, trying to block out the sounds of a baby crying in the waiting room and construction workers chanting reasonable demands outside, that poetry would not save my life, as I had expected, in the end, it would. On the contrary, sitting there I realized that something called "poetry," loosely sketched from what I imagined that word to mean when I was a teenager, maybe a water tower with a tree growing from its roof on a fascist's private property, might in fact at some point down the road play a hand in killing me. But what, I thought, if I were to put it in prose? I sighed. "What's that about?" my therapist said. An image of a pane of broken glass in the middle of a meadow in Seven Springs flashed through my mind. No, prose wouldn't work either. I answered, not meaning to sound cold, "I wouldn't put it that way."

5.

Chris and I walked into Katie's bookstore and tried to ratchet our faces into a humane muscular arrangement. It had been a terrible morning. Earlier, moments before I stepped up for my poetry reading at the local Episcopalian church, I checked my phone and saw, in sickening shock, that C., a poet and orga- nizer from back in New York with whom I was friendly but not particularly close, had been killed by her male roommate the night before. In an article that morning the *New York Post* had identified C. as "a waitress struggling to pay the rent," and her killer as a "struggling artist." I read through posts from our mutual friends who had known her better than I had; one posted a picture of a plant that she had named after C. upon hearing the news; I thought I might cry, then found I couldn't. A few brief sequences from the previous year played on loops through my head as I sat there staring at my phone: C. sitting down next to me at a reading where no one else would talk to me and striking up a conversation; dancing with her to a Robyn song in a crowded loft while snow fell outside near the Navy

Yard; bumming a cigarette from her outside a bar, exchanging a grin, and walking home without knowing that this would be the last time I saw her. I showed Chris my phone and he gaped in disbelief, and I fell numb. I knew I had to say something about it to the small festival crowd assembled before me, and as I heard my name announced and I walked up to the pulpit, I felt my limbs fill with the soothing rage that presages disastrous public speech. But when I looked out over the pews I couldn't do it–it would only have alienated the audience and made them feel terrible, and I was too angry to make my point. I thanked the festival for bringing me and forced my way through an excerpt of a long, autobiographical haibun called "A View of Vesuvius" while three people openly fell asleep in front of me. It was the worst reading I've ever given. When I finished a local senior poet smiled and told me that my poem was "very interesting" but that my reading voice was "too casual." Chris hugged me as people milled around. No one else in Harbor Springs ever found out about what had happened the night before in Brooklyn. Back in the bookstore Katie leveled a patient smile in our direction from behind the register as we entered. She was nine months pregnant, nary a sign of strain on her face, though she was running a book festival and a store while on the verge of going into labor. I realized that despite the fact that we had once been close, I now knew very little about her life. She asked me how the reading went; I said it had been great. We told her about the car and what the mechanic had told us, and she chuckled and said, "Look at these jackasses rolling into town in a foreign car!" We all laughed, but it wasn't clear for whom she'd made this joke. "No, but seriously, I'm so sorry–that's

terrible." She offered to help us expedite a new catalytic con-
verter from Detroit; her husband's father was in the auto in-
dustry and could make a call for us if we wanted. Chris perked
up. "That would be incredible," he said. A flat expression
passed over her face, and she began muttering that it might
actually be too much trouble. We all stood there awkwardly for
a moment, not quite understanding one another, but for me
and Chris her meaning quickly crystallized: we had not fol-
lowed the dance. Chris was supposed to say, "Thank you, that's
very kind, but we'll find our way out of this." We immediately
backpedaled, practically falling over ourselves to assure her it
would be no problem at all; we would wait to see what the me-
chanic said. She nodded gravely. I felt a pale root inside me
choking under a thick, affable topsoil. Katie said we should
come over for dinner that night—nothing fancy, but they would
love to have us. We thanked her and said we would love that
too. Chris and I walked back outside and stared over the lake.
It had stopped raining. Katie's dinner was delicious. In the end
the catalytic converter arrived early. We ordered Jim and Laurie
autumn tulips, bought several books from Katie at her store,
and only missed two days of work.

6.

"I thought of a way to title poems," I said to Callie. "It's called
the Hell Test. It goes like this. If you're writing in the present
tense and you're trying to find a title for a poem, you need to
first ask yourself if the events in your poem might plausibly be
able to fall under the title 'Hell.' If yes, there you go—you should

call your poem 'Hell.' If no, you then need to ask yourself if there is another title for this particular poem that could plausibly serve better, or at least more troublingly, more ornately troublingly, as a title—something like 'Night Smell' or 'The Thorn of the Night Smell.' And if you can't think of anything that good, you know what to do. Just call your poem 'Hell.'" Callie looked up from her tablet and rubbed her eyes. "Would it work for novels too?" she said. "Yes, especially for novels," I said. She looked out the window at the glowing red clock hands blazing through the night at the top of the bank tower, the tallest building in Brooklyn, then back at me. "What if you're not writing in the present tense?"

7.

The vacant stars are not enough, nor the gravity of one's parents. The last time I went to Seven Springs I entered the meadow as I had for years, stuck by the low idling of the property, my blood rumbling among weaponized flowers. I wanted to see this one part of the field, the pane of glass installed over a chimney running into the ground. I walked up to peek in, but as I approached through the grass something seemed wrong. I believe in the reality of absent things; if something isn't there I assume it must be somewhere else. The glass had cracked, and more than half the pane was gone. This is why we need poetry, because in the end no prose can absorb the shrillness of what I couldn't see there. It was too dark below, so I walked around to a hatch, pulled it open, felt the damp air creep up, and, after some heavy hesitation, entered. I saw paw prints and little piles of scat at the foot of the latch. These I will not forget. I walked down the stairs. The air was damp and thick with a richer mineral than I could name. Moisture dripped from a small rusted tank. The back of my scalp tingled. This is about more than who owned the deed, but that was the worst part yet–I was under purchased earth, and everything was open. And while I knew that something even more awful was coming soon, I felt happy. I looked down at my feet. In the shadow six inches off lay a dead coyote. He was drenched and had entered from above. But this is not about the material he fell through. His eyes

were still cracked open
I stepped back, then stepped forward
and this is what he said

ACKNOWLEDGMENTS

Many of these poems were previously published, often in early forms: "Red Sea" (the *PoetryNow* podcast from the Poetry Foundation); "Rumors" (*The Fanzine*); "Dumpster" (*Kenyon Review*); "Aries" (*Bennington Review*); "Ecstatic Zero" (*Hyperallergic*); "A View of Vesuvius" and "Fear of Description" (*BOMB*); "The Art Buyer" (*PEN Poetry Series*); "The Hell Test (Seven Springs)" (*Yale Review*). "Rumors" also appears in the anthology *Ritual and Capital* from Wendy's Subway. My thanks to all of the editors of these journals, past and present, especially Raluca Albu, Andrew Bourne, Michael Dumanis, Regan Good, Andrew Grace, Gabe Kruis, David Lynn, Chantal McStay, Maggie Millner, Meghan O'Rourke, Kirsten Reach, Danniel Schoonebeek, Michael Slosek, Mónica de la Torre, Rachel Valinsky, and Wendy Xu.

A residency at the Norton Island colony provided crucial support while I was writing many of these poems—my thanks to the Eastern Frontier Educational Foundation and to Steve Dunn. My thanks also to Rusty Morrison; to Katie Capaldi, Jim Ford, and Laurie Ford; to Jill Schoolman and Kendall Storey; to Anne Flick; to all my former bookseller colleagues at Book-Court; to my colleagues at 92Y; to Paul Slovak and everyone at Penguin; to Beth Dial and everyone at the National Poetry Series; to the Lannan Foundation; to Jennifer Moxley; and especially to Brenda Shaughnessy.

Conversations, correspondences, and convivial shit-talking with a number of beloved friends provided invaluable encouragement and insight while I was writing and editing this book, especially Sara Deniz Akant, Rawaan Alkhatib, Micah Bateman, Brandon Brown, Ashley Colley, Sophia Dahlin, Brittany Denison, Farnoosh Fathi, Jake Fournier, Katie Fowley, Adjua Greaves, Gillian Olivia Blythe Hamel, Mike Lala, Ariel Lewiton, Emily Liebowitz, Eric Linsker, Rachel Mannheimer, Chris Martin, Ted Mathys, Mark Mayer, Andrés Millan, Sara Nicholson, Zachary Pace, Hilary Plum, Kristen Radtke, Adrienne Raphel, Margaret Ross, Zach Savich, Rob Schlegel, Natalie Shapero, Emily Skillings, Colby Somerville, Mary Austin Speaker, Bridget Talone, Nick Twemlow, G. C. Waldrep, Noah Warren, Lisa Wells, Eric Dean Wilson, and Rebecca Zweig–my profound gratitude to all of you.

My thanks to Molly Boylan, Christian Garnett, Jean Garnett, and Nick Kinsey; and to my parents, my brother, and my sister for their collective spark, generosity, patience, warmth, and support.

Callie Garnett, David Gorin, Jessica Laser, and Christian Schlegel made writing this book possible. "And I am lost without you."

NOTES

"Aries": "'As love requires a politics, worldliness cathects'" (Lisa Robertson); "Over a number of years you behave in so many ways that in the end / No matter what people say of you, they're right" (Jake Fournier, in conversation).

"A View of Vesuvius": "'We tooth fairies are part of a union'" (ASMRrequests); "the Elizabethans called it dying" (James Schuyler); the "song my grandfather used to sing when he was happy" is "Goin' Back to Where I Come From," a traditional folk song tracked down by my vigilant copy editor in the final stages of editing, for which I am very grateful; the terminal haiku of this poem paraphrases part of Springbok ASMR's *Binaural ASMR Poetry Reading with Commentary* (May 27, 2014), available on YouTube.

"The Art Buyer": A number of lines in this poem make reference to or directly quote *Paradise Lost* and *The Tempest*; a number of lines quote Austrian ethologist Karl von Frisch's *The Dancing Bees* (1953), an account of von Frisch's research into various modes of perception and communication in honeybee populations. The phrase "Roman air" is from W. H. Auden's "Anthem for St. Cecilia's Day." This poem is dedicated to Andrés Millan, in memory of Juan Daniel Millan.

■

The long poems in this book–particularly the haibun–were deeply informed by four texts that are not directly cited herein.

Dana Ward's "Typing 'Wild Speech'" from *This Can't Be Life* (Edge Books, 2012) mapped out new possibilities for me in both the prose poem and the elegy; Jennifer Moxley's memoir *The Middle Room* (Subpress, 2007) crystallized an intuition that poetry is the sum of a collective act, and that it corresponds with friendship; Christian Schlegel's haibun series provided the initial spark for "A View of Vesuvius" and "Rumors," and inspired a first reading of Bashō's seminal work in the form, *Oku no Hosomichi* (translated into English as *The Narrow Road to Oku, The Narrow Road to the North, Back Roads through Small Towns*, etc.), another crucial text; and Chris's great long poem "Michigan"—which was the impetus for "The Hell Test (Seven Springs)" and contains a more detailed account of the road trip referenced in that poem—was equally inspiring.

PENGUIN POETS